MARY MARCUS

The life of St. Frances of Rome

Copyright © 2023 by Mary Marcus

All rights reserved. No part of this publication may be reproduced, stored or transmitted in any form or by any means, electronic, mechanical, photocopying, recording, scanning, or otherwise without written permission from the publisher. It is illegal to copy this book, post it to a website, or distribute it by any other means without permission.

First edition

*This book was professionally typeset on Reedsy.
Find out more at reedsy.com*

Contents

1 Introduction   1
2 Devotion and Spirituality   5
3 Charitable Works   12
4 Life Challenges   21
5 Canonization and Legacy   28
6 Patronage and Feast Day   37
7 Complete Novena   44
8 Conclusion   57

1

Introduction

Background and Early Life

St. Frances of Rome, born on January 1384 into a noble Roman family, experienced a childhood marked by privilege and affluence. Raised amidst the social elite, her family's prominence allowed her access to education and cultural refinement. The atmosphere of medieval Rome provided a backdrop of political and religious intrigue, influencing young Frances even in her formative years.

Despite the external glamour, Frances exhibited a distinct spiritual inclination from an early age. Her religious fervor often set her apart, as she demonstrated a deep compassion for the less fortunate, even in her youth. This early compassion sowed the seeds for her future endeavors in charitable works.

As Frances matured, her parents arranged a marriage to Lorenzo Ponziani, a marriage seen as advantageous for both families. This union, however, did not diminish Frances' commitment to her faith. In fact, marriage became a means through which she could channel her religious devotion, blending the secular responsibilities of family life with a profound commitment to God.

This period of her life marked the intersection of worldly expectations and Frances' growing spiritual consciousness. It set the stage for the transformative journey that would lead her to establish a religious community dedicated to serving the marginalized, a testament to her unwavering dedication to both her familial duties and her profound faith.

Historical Context

St. Frances of Rome lived during a crucial period of history, where the political, social, and religious landscapes of medieval Europe underwent significant transformations. The late 14th century in Italy, the time of Frances' birth, was marked by a complex interplay of events that shaped the context of her life.

Medieval Rome:

Frances was born into the heart of medieval Rome, a city characterized by its rich history, ecclesiastical power, and political intrigue. The Papal States, ruled by the Pope, played a central role in the city's governance, influencing both spiritual and secular affairs.

Religious Dynamics:

The Church held immense influence over the lives of individuals during this period. The Catholic Church was not only a spiritual authority but also a political force, with popes often entangled in power struggles and conflicts.

Social Disparities:

The societal structure was hierarchical, with clear divisions between the aristocracy and common people. Frances' noble background placed her among the privileged class, allowing her unique insights into the socio-economic disparities of the time.

Challenges and Turmoil:

The 14th century witnessed challenges such as the Black Death, which brought widespread death and societal upheaval. These difficulties tested the resilience of individuals and communities, fostering a climate where acts of charity and compassion were both essential and impactful.

Renaissance Influences:

The Renaissance was dawning, characterized by a renewed interest in art, culture, and humanism. While Frances lived on the cusp of this cultural renaissance, her life primarily reflected the religious piety and charitable ideals associated with the preceding medieval era.

Understanding this historical context is crucial for appreciating the choices and actions of St. Frances of Rome, as she navigated a world shaped by both the turbulence of her time and the timeless spiritual values that guided her life's journey.

2

Devotion and Spirituality

Early Signs of Devotion

St. Frances of Rome's spiritual journey was evident from her earliest years, displaying signs of devotion that set her apart even in her youth. These early indications of her profound faith and dedication to God foreshadowed the remarkable path she would later tread.

Childhood Piety:

Even as a child amidst the luxuries of her noble upbringing, Frances exhibited an innate sense of piety. She was often drawn to prayer and contemplation, displaying a maturity and depth of spiritual understanding beyond her years.

Compassion for the Poor:

Frances' heart was deeply touched by the suffering of the less fortunate. From a young age, she showed a remarkable sensitivity to the needs of the poor, often using her resources to assist them, reflecting the teachings of Christ to serve the least among us.

Spiritual Disciplines:

Early on, Frances embraced spiritual disciplines with fervor. She dedicated time to reading sacred texts, attending Mass, and participating in religious rituals, cultivating a personal relationship with God that anchored her life.

Visions and Mystical Experiences:

Frances' spiritual experiences were not confined to conventional practices. She began to have visions and mystical encounters from a young age, offering her glimpses into the divine and reinforcing her commitment to a life of holiness.

Influence of Spiritual Mentors:

Recognizing her deep devotion, spiritual guides and mentors played a pivotal role in nurturing Frances' faith. Their influence helped shape her spiritual path, providing guidance and encouragement as she embarked on her journey of devotion.

These early signs of devotion in St. Frances of Rome were not mere fleeting moments but rather foundational elements that shaped her character and guided her actions throughout her life. They underscored her unwavering commitment to God and set the stage for her future endeavors in service and holiness.

Spiritual Practices and Prayer Life

St. Frances of Rome's life was characterized by a rich tapestry of spiritual practices and a deeply committed prayer life. These elements were integral to her identity as a devout Christian and were instrumental in shaping her connection with the divine.

Liturgy and Mass Attendance:

Central to Frances' spiritual routine was active participation in liturgical practices. Attending Mass regularly, she found solace and communion with God through the sacred rituals of the Church, drawing strength from the Eucharist.

Daily Prayer and Contemplation:

Frances cultivated a habit of daily prayer and contemplation. Her prayer life extended beyond formal rituals, encompassing intimate conversations with God. This contemplative dimension allowed her to deepen her relationship with the divine and seek guidance in her daily challenges.

Scripture Reading and Reflection:

A voracious reader of sacred texts, Frances immersed herself in the wisdom of the Scriptures. Regular engagement with the Word of God served as a source of inspiration and guidance, shaping her understanding of Christian virtues and moral principles.

Acts of Charity as Prayer:

For Frances, acts of charity were a profound expression of prayer. Her service to the poor and sick was not merely a duty but a form of worship. She embraced the teachings of Christ, viewing compassionate actions as a direct channel to connect with the divine.

Silent Retreats and Solitude:

Understanding the value of solitude, Frances embarked on silent retreats. These periods of withdrawal allowed her to delve deeper into her spiritual journey, fostering a contemplative atmosphere where she could listen more attentively to the promptings of the Holy Spirit.

Guidance from Spiritual Directors:

Recognizing the importance of spiritual guidance, Frances sought counsel from trusted mentors. Spiritual directors played a crucial role in shaping her prayer life, providing insights and encouragement as she navigated the complexities of her spiritual path.

Mystical Experiences and Visions:

Frances' prayer life was enriched by mystical experiences and divine visions. These encounters with the transcendent not only deepened her faith but also served as a source of inspiration for her charitable works and devotion to God.

St. Frances of Rome's spiritual practices and prayer life were intertwined, forming a harmonious rhythm that sustained her through a life dedicated to God and the service of others. Her example continues to inspire believers to cultivate a vibrant and meaningful relationship with the divine through prayer and devotion.

Mystical Experiences and Visions

St. Frances of Rome's spiritual journey was punctuated by mystical experiences and divine visions, elevating her connection with the divine to extraordinary heights. These encounters played a profound role in shaping her faith and influencing her actions throughout her life.

Early Visions as a Child:

Frances' mystical experiences commenced in her early years. As a child, she reported having visions that provided glimpses into the spiritual realm. These extraordinary encounters fueled her innate sense of devotion and set the stage for a life marked by divine communication.

Heavenly Insights during Prayer:

In the solitude of prayer, Frances often received heavenly insights and profound revelations. These moments of divine communion deepened her understanding of God's will and infused her with a sense of purpose, guiding her actions in the service of others.

Guidance in Times of Decision:

Throughout her life, Frances turned to divine guidance during critical junctures. Her mystical experiences offered clarity and direction, especially in moments of decision-making, reinforcing her belief that a life aligned with God's will was the path to true fulfillment.

Visions of Angels and Saints:

Frances reported visions of angels and saints, testifying to her heightened spiritual sensitivity. These encounters provided comfort and inspiration, affirming the interconnectedness of the earthly and heavenly realms in her spiritual journey.

Ecstatic Experiences in Prayer:

During intense periods of prayer and contemplation, Frances experienced moments of ecstasy. These transcendent states allowed her to transcend the limitations of the material world, experiencing a profound union with God that fueled her commitment to a life of holiness.

Prophetic Insights:

Frances' mystical experiences often contained elements of prophecy. She would receive insights into future events or a deeper understanding of the spiritual significance of unfolding circumstances, reinforcing her role as a conduit for divine wisdom.

Visions of the Crucified Christ:

A central theme in Frances' mystical encounters was visions of the Crucified Christ. These experiences of contemplating the suffering of Christ profoundly impacted her spirituality, deepening her empathy for the suffering of humanity and inspiring her charitable works.

Silent Conversations with the Virgin Mary:

Frances reported silent conversations with the Virgin Mary, experiencing a unique bond with the Mother of God. These exchanges provided solace and strength, reinforcing her sense of divine companionship in her earthly journey.

St. Frances of Rome's mystical experiences and visions added a transcendent dimension to her spirituality, shaping her as a mystic and guiding her in her mission of service and devotion to God. These encounters continue to captivate the imaginations of those who seek a deeper connection with the divine.

3

Charitable Works

Foundation of the Community

St. Frances of Rome's commitment to a life of service and devotion to God found concrete expression in the foundation of a religious community. This community, known as the Oblates of Mary, became a testament to her vision of combining contemplative spirituality with active charity.

Inspiration from Divine Prompting:

Frances' decision to establish a religious community was inspired by what she perceived as a divine calling. Through her mystical experiences and prayer life, she felt a compelling inner guidance urging her to create a community dedicated to serving the needs of the poor and sick.

Oblates of Mary:

In 1425, with the support of her husband Lorenzo, Frances

founded the Oblates of Mary. This religious community was unique in its blending of monastic principles with an active commitment to charitable works. Members, while embracing a contemplative life, also engaged in practical service to those in need.

Charism and Rule of Life:

Frances crafted a distinct charism and rule of life for the community, outlining the principles that would guide its members. The rule emphasized a balance between contemplative prayer, community life, and active works of mercy, reflecting Frances' holistic approach to spirituality.

Community Life in Rome:

The Oblates of Mary established their community in Rome, where they lived in simplicity and shared a communal life. This environment fostered a sense of sisterhood and mutual support among the members, creating a space where spiritual growth and charitable service could coexist.

Combining Contemplation and Action:
   One of the unique aspects of Frances' community was its intentional integration of contemplative practices with active service. The members devoted time to prayer, Eucharistic adoration, and spiritual readings, while also engaging in hands-on care for the less fortunate.

Works of Mercy:

The Oblates of Mary, under Frances' guidance, actively participated in various works of mercy. This included providing assistance to the sick, feeding the hungry, and offering support to those in need. Their charitable activities extended beyond the convent walls, reaching out to the marginalized in the broader community.

Legacy of Charity:

Frances' foundation laid the groundwork for a lasting legacy of charity. The Oblates of Mary continued her mission long after her death, perpetuating her vision of a community that embodied the compassionate teachings of Christ.

The foundation of the Oblates of Mary was a manifestation of St. Frances of Rome's desire to bridge the gap between the contemplative and active aspects of religious life. Through this community, she created a lasting institution that would carry on her legacy of devotion to God and service to humanity.

Mission and Objectives

The mission and objectives of the Oblates of Mary, founded by St. Frances of Rome, were rooted in a profound commitment to holiness, charity, and the service of God through practical works of mercy.

Mission:

The overarching mission of the Oblates of Mary was to live

a life dedicated to God's service, seeking holiness through a harmonious blend of contemplative prayer and active charitable works. The community aimed to embody the teachings of Christ, particularly the call to love and serve the least among us.

Objectives:

Contemplative Prayer and Adoration:

Foster a deep life of prayer and contemplation, with a special emphasis on Eucharistic adoration.

Cultivate a personal and communal relationship with God through regular prayer and spiritual exercises.

Living a Life of Virtue:

Embrace a virtuous life, following the example of Christ and the teachings of the Gospel.
   Strive for personal holiness and spiritual growth through the practice of virtues such as humility, charity, and obedience.

Active Works of Mercy:

Engage in active charitable works to meet the practical needs of the poor, sick, and marginalized.

Provide assistance, comfort, and care to those facing various forms of suffering and adversity.

Community Life and Mutual Support:

Build a strong sense of community among members, fostering a supportive environment for spiritual growth.

Encourage mutual support and collaboration in both prayer and charitable activities.

Education and Spiritual Formation:

Prioritize ongoing spiritual formation for community members, ensuring a deep understanding of the Christian faith.

Provide opportunities for education and training to equip members for effective service in their charitable endeavors.

Obedience to the Rule and Charism:

Adhere faithfully to the established rule of life and charism of the community, as outlined by St. Frances of Rome.

Uphold the distinctive characteristics that define the Oblates of Mary, maintaining the balance between contemplation and action.

Outreach and Evangelization:

Extend the community's reach beyond the convent walls to positively impact the broader community.

Share the message of God's love and the transformative power of a life lived in accordance with Christian principles.

Adaptability and Responsiveness:

Remain adaptable to the changing needs of society, adjusting charitable efforts to address evolving challenges.

Respond to the promptings of the Holy Spirit in discerning new ways to fulfill the mission of the community.

By aligning their mission with these objectives, the Oblates of Mary sought to perpetuate the spiritual legacy of St. Frances of Rome, embodying a holistic approach to religious life that combined devotion to God with a fervent commitment to serving others.

Outreach to the Poor and Sick

The Oblates of Mary, guided by the vision of St. Frances of Rome, undertook a compassionate and hands-on approach in their outreach to the poor and sick. This aspect of their mission was a direct reflection of their commitment to living out the teachings of Christ through practical acts of mercy.

Personalized Care and Compassion:

Members of the Oblates of Mary actively engaged with individuals in need, offering personalized care and demonstrating genuine compassion.

The community emphasized the importance of recognizing the inherent dignity of each person, fostering a spirit of empathy in their interactions.

Home Visits and Hospital Ministry:

Community members regularly conducted home visits to families facing economic hardships, providing material assistance and emotional support.

Hospital ministry was a significant component of their outreach, where they offered comfort and care to the sick, embodying the healing ministry of Christ.

Material Assistance and Basic Needs:

The Oblates of Mary addressed immediate needs by providing material assistance such as food, clothing, and shelter to those struggling with poverty.

They recognized the importance of meeting basic needs as a foundational step towards empowering individuals to overcome challenging circumstances.

Advocacy for the Vulnerable:

The community actively advocated for the rights and well-being of the vulnerable in society, amplifying the voices of those marginalized by poverty and illness.

Their advocacy extended beyond immediate relief efforts, seeking systemic change to address the root causes of social injustices.

Spiritual Comfort and Counseling:

In addition to physical care, the Oblates of Mary offered spiritual comfort and counseling to those facing emotional and psychological challenges.

Their commitment to holistic well-being encompassed addressing both the material and spiritual dimensions of individuals' lives.

Empowerment through Education:

Recognizing the transformative power of education, the community initiated programs to empower individuals and families to break the cycle of poverty.

Educational initiatives focused on providing practical skills and knowledge to enhance the long-term prospects of those they served.

Community-Based Initiatives:

The Oblates of Mary actively engaged with local communities, establishing programs that fostered a sense of solidarity and mutual support.

Initiatives included community gardens, skill development workshops, and other projects aimed at building resilience within marginalized communities.

End-of-Life Care and Bereavement Support:

Acknowledging the dignity of life until its natural end, the community offered end-of-life care to the terminally ill.

Bereavement support services were provided to families, recognizing the importance of accompanying them through the difficult process of loss.

Through these diverse outreach efforts, the Oblates of Mary exemplified a holistic and Christ-centered approach to charity. Their commitment to the poor and sick went beyond immediate relief, aiming to restore dignity, foster empowerment, and embody the transformative love of God in tangible ways.

4

Life Challenges

Personal Struggles and Sacrifices

St. Frances of Rome, despite her noble upbringing and spiritual devotion, encountered personal struggles and made significant sacrifices throughout her life in pursuit of her religious calling.

Marital Obligations:

Frances' marriage to Lorenzo Ponziani, while arranged for familial advantages, initially presented challenges as she sought to balance her matrimonial duties with her deep spiritual yearnings.

Her commitment to family life did not deter her from embracing a devout Christian existence, navigating the tensions between worldly expectations and her spiritual aspirations.

Loss and Grief:

Frances experienced the profound grief of losing her children. The deaths of her children were emotionally taxing, testing her resilience and faith in the face of personal tragedy.

Enduring such losses became a testament to her strength and unwavering commitment to her religious vocation.

Opposition and Criticism:

The establishment of the Oblates of Mary faced opposition and criticism, both within and outside the Church. Some questioned the unconventional combination of contemplative and active life embraced by the community.

Frances endured skepticism and resistance with patience, steadfastly adhering to her convictions despite external challenges.

Health Struggles:

Frances faced health challenges that included physical ailments, which added an extra layer of difficulty to her daily life and religious duties.

Her perseverance through physical trials demonstrated a resilience that mirrored her spiritual strength.

Balancing Contemplation and Action:

The Oblates of Mary's unique approach of combining contemplative prayer with active works of mercy required a delicate balance. Frances navigated the tension between the solitude of contemplation and the demands of hands-on charitable service.

Striking this balance demanded sacrifices as she dedicated herself to both prayerful communion with God and practical care for those in need.

Financial Strain:

The Oblates of Mary, committed to serving the poor, often faced financial challenges in sustaining their charitable initiatives.

Frances, having come from a privileged background, embraced a life that required financial sacrifices, redirecting resources toward the community's mission rather than personal comfort.

Misunderstandings within the Community:

Internal challenges within the community occasionally led to misunderstandings and conflicts among its members.

Frances, as a leader, navigated these challenges with humility and patience, fostering a spirit of unity and mutual understanding within the community.

Enduring Criticism for Mystical Experiences:

Frances' mystical experiences and visions were met with skepticism and criticism by some contemporaries who questioned the authenticity of her encounters with the divine.

Enduring such skepticism required Frances to rely on her deep faith and inner conviction, trusting in the authenticity of her spiritual experiences.

St. Frances of Rome's life was not exempt from personal struggles and sacrifices, yet her unwavering commitment to her religious calling allowed her to transcend these challenges. Through resilience and faith, she navigated a path marked by both personal difficulties and profound spiritual fulfillment.

Opposition and Criticisms

St. Frances of Rome faced opposition and criticisms throughout her life, particularly in relation to the establishment of the Oblates of Mary and her unique approach to combining contemplative and active religious life.

Unconventional Charism:

The charism and rule of life set forth by St. Frances for the Oblates of Mary were considered unconventional and even controversial by some within the Church.

Critics questioned the feasibility of seamlessly blending contemplative prayer with active engagement in charitable works, challenging traditional views on monastic life.

Resistance within the Church:

Within the ecclesiastical hierarchy, there was resistance to Frances' vision for the Oblates of Mary. Some clergy and religious authorities were skeptical about the viability and orthodoxy of the community's unique structure.

Frances had to navigate bureaucratic obstacles and convince ecclesiastical leaders of the legitimacy of her charism.

Distrust of Mystical Experiences:

Frances' mystical experiences and visions faced skepticism and distrust from those who questioned the authenticity of her encounters with the divine.

Some members of the Church hierarchy and the wider community were hesitant to accept the validity of her spiritual revelations, leading to ongoing scrutiny and suspicion.

Financial Challenges:

The community's commitment to serving the poor and marginalized faced financial challenges, with critics questioning the sustainability of their charitable initiatives.

Skeptics argued that the unique combination of contemplative life and active charity might not be financially viable in the long term.

Social Stigma:

The blending of a noblewoman's life with a commitment to a religious community and service to the poor defied societal norms of the time.

Frances faced social stigma from those who found her unconventional choices and lifestyle difficult to reconcile with prevailing expectations for women of her status.

Criticism of Female Leadership:

As a female religious leader in a time when women's roles were often limited, Frances faced criticism for her leadership of the Oblates of Mary.

Some questioned the legitimacy of a woman assuming a central role in the foundation and governance of a religious community.

Challenges to the Rule of Life:

The rule of life set by Frances for the Oblates of Mary, which emphasized a unique combination of contemplation and action, was met with skepticism.

Critics argued that this blending of monastic and active elements might dilute the rigor and spiritual depth traditionally associated with monastic life.

Internal Conflicts:

The community itself experienced internal conflicts and challenges as members adapted to the distinctive charism outlined by Frances.

Managing internal dissent and fostering unity required Frances to address and navigate disagreements within the community.

Despite facing opposition and criticisms, St. Frances of Rome remained steadfast in her commitment to the mission of the Oblates of Mary. Her resilience and conviction ultimately contributed to the acceptance and flourishing of the community, demonstrating the transformative power of her vision.

5

Canonization and Legacy

Process of Canonization

The canonization of St. Frances of Rome was a meticulous and multi-stage process undertaken by the Catholic Church to officially recognize her as a saint. The canonization process typically involves several steps:

Local Recognition:

Initially, the local community recognizes an individual's sanctity and begins to venerate them as a holy person. This grassroots devotion often serves as the starting point for the canonization process.

Appointment of a Postulator:

A postulator is appointed to advocate for the cause of canonization. This individual is responsible for gathering evidence of the candidate's holiness, virtue, and the impact of their life.

Opening of the Cause:

The diocesan bishop, with the guidance of the postulator, officially opens the cause for canonization. This involves a thorough investigation into the life, writings, and reputation of the candidate.

Declaration of Servant of God:

After a positive assessment of the candidate's life, the individual is declared a "Servant of God." This declaration signifies that the Church acknowledges the person's exceptional holiness and allows for a deeper examination of their life.

Positio:

The postulator compiles a detailed document called the "Positio," presenting evidence supporting the candidate's virtues, miracles, and impact on the Church. This document is submitted to the Vatican's Congregation for the Causes of Saints.

Theological Examination:

The Positio undergoes a theological examination by a panel of experts within the Congregation for the Causes of Saints. This examination assesses the candidate's adherence to Christian doctrine and the theological significance of their life.

Approval by Theologians and Cardinals:

If the theologians and cardinals within the congregation find the Positio satisfactory, they recommend the candidate for beatification and, subsequently, canonization. The Pope may then issue a decree recognizing the heroic virtues of the Servant of God.

Beatification:

Beatification is the next step in the process. The Pope declares the individual "Blessed," acknowledging that the person is in heaven and worthy of veneration. Beatification usually requires the confirmation of one miracle attributed to the intercession of the Blessed.

Second Miracle and Canonization:

For canonization, a second miracle is typically required. After the confirmation of the second miracle, the Pope can proceed to canonize the individual, officially declaring them a saint.

Proclamation of Sainthood:

The canonization ceremony is a public proclamation of the individual's sainthood. It includes the formal reading of the canonization decree, the singing of the Litany of the Saints, and the Pope's declaration that the new saint is to be venerated by the universal Church.

St. Frances of Rome underwent this rigorous process, with her canonization occurring on May 29, 1608, when Pope Paul V officially recognized her as a saint. Her life and virtues continue to inspire believers, and her feast day is celebrated annually on

March 9th.

Recognition as a Saint

St. Frances of Rome's recognition as a saint within the Catholic Church was a culmination of a thorough process that acknowledged her exemplary life and holiness. The steps leading to her recognition included:

Local Veneration:

St. Frances of Rome's journey to sainthood began with local recognition and veneration by the faithful. Her holiness and the impact of her life became evident within the community where she lived and served.

Appointment of Postulators:

Postulators, individuals appointed to champion the cause of canonization, played a crucial role. They were tasked with gathering evidence of Frances' sanctity, virtues, and the impact of her life.

Opening of the Cause:

The diocesan bishop, under the guidance of the postulator, officially opened the cause for canonization. This initiated a thorough investigation into Frances' life, examining her writings, virtues, and reputation for holiness.

Declaration as Servant of God:

Following a positive assessment, St. Frances of Rome was declared a "Servant of God." This designation acknowledged her exceptional holiness and paved the way for a more detailed examination of her life.

Positio:

The postulator compiled the "Positio," a comprehensive document presenting evidence supporting Frances' virtues, holiness, and the impact of her life. This document was submitted to the Vatican's Congregation for the Causes of Saints.

Theological Examination:

The Positio underwent theological scrutiny by a panel of experts within the Congregation for the Causes of Saints. This examination assessed the theological significance of Frances' life and her adherence to Christian doctrine.

Approval by Theologians and Cardinals:

Theologians and cardinals within the congregation, upon finding the Positio satisfactory, recommended Frances for beatification and canonization. Their approval signaled recognition of her heroic virtues.

Beatification:

Pope Paul V beatified St. Frances of Rome on November 9, 1608, declaring her "Blessed." This step acknowledged her presence in heaven and her eligibility for veneration.

Second Miracle and Canonization:

To proceed to canonization, a second miracle attributed to Frances' intercession was required. The confirmation of this second miracle provided the basis for Pope Paul V to canonize her.

Proclamation of Sainthood:

On May 29, 1608, Pope Paul V officially declared St. Frances of Rome a saint in a canonization ceremony. This proclamation acknowledged her as a model of Christian virtue and holiness, and she was included in the list of saints to be venerated by the universal Church.

St. Frances of Rome's recognition as a saint solidified her place in the Catholic liturgical calendar, and her life continues to inspire believers as they commemorate her feast day on March 9th each year.

Impact and Influence

St. Frances of Rome's impact and influence extend beyond her historical context, leaving a lasting legacy that resonates in the hearts of believers and the broader Catholic Church.

Charitable Inspiration:

St. Frances of Rome's commitment to serving the poor and sick has inspired countless individuals to emulate her charitable spirit. Her life serves as a beacon for those seeking to make a tangible difference in the lives of others through acts of mercy and compassion.

Model of Holiness:

As a canonized saint, Frances stands as a model of holiness and virtue. Her dedication to a life of prayer, contemplation, and active charity provides a template for spiritual seekers striving for deeper communion with God while engaging in the world.

Founding the Oblates of Mary:

The religious community founded by Frances, the Oblates of Mary, continues to exist and carry out its mission of combining contemplative life with active works of mercy. The community's enduring presence is a testament to Frances' vision and the sustainability of her innovative approach to religious life.

Influence on Religious Communities:

Frances' unique model of blending contemplation with active service has influenced other religious communities and individuals seeking a balanced approach to spirituality. Her example challenges the perception that a life of deep prayer and engagement with the world are mutually exclusive.

Patronage of Motorists and Widows:

St. Frances of Rome is recognized as the patron saint of motorists and widows. Her intercession is sought for the safety of those on the road and for the well-being of widows. This patronage underscores her connection to everyday aspects of life and the concerns of various communities.

Spiritual Writings:

Frances' spiritual writings, including her reflections and insights on prayer and devotion, continue to be a source of inspiration. Her works offer guidance to those navigating the spiritual journey and seeking a deeper connection with God.

Recognition in Liturgy:

The inclusion of St. Frances of Rome in the liturgical calendar ensures that her life and contributions are commemorated annually. Her feast day, celebrated on March 9th, provides an opportunity for the faithful to reflect on her legacy and seek her intercession.

Educational and Charitable Institutions:

Various educational and charitable institutions, named in honor of St. Frances of Rome, stand as a testament to her enduring impact. These institutions continue her legacy by embodying the values of compassion, service, and holistic education.

St. Frances of Rome's influence transcends time, offering a profound example of how a life dedicated to God and the service of others can leave an indelible mark on individuals and communities. Her legacy challenges and inspires, inviting others to embrace a spirituality that bridges the sacred and the secular.

6

Patronage and Feast Day

Designation as Patron Saint

St. Frances of Rome received special designations as the patron saint for specific groups and concerns, reflecting the recognition of her intercessory power and connection to various aspects of life.

Patron Saint of Motorists:

St. Frances of Rome is widely recognized as the patron saint of motorists. The designation acknowledges her role as a protector for those traveling on the roads, seeking her intercession for safety and guidance during journeys.

Patron Saint of Widows:

Frances holds the title of patron saint of widows. This designation reflects her empathy and understanding of the challenges faced by widowed individuals. Widows turn to her for comfort, solace, and assistance in navigating the difficulties that accompany the loss of a spouse.

These specific designations highlight the broad reach of St. Frances of Rome's intercessory influence, encompassing both practical aspects of daily life, such as travel safety, and the emotional and spiritual support needed by widows facing the unique challenges of bereavement. Her patronage serves as a reminder of her enduring impact on the lives of diverse communities and individuals.

Celebration of Feast Day

The celebration of St. Frances of Rome's feast day, observed annually on March 9th, is a joyous occasion for the Catholic Church and those inspired by her life. The commemoration involves various elements that honor her contributions and virtues:

Mass and Liturgical Celebrations:

The feast day begins with special Masses celebrated in churches around the world. These liturgical services focus on St. Frances of Rome's life, holiness, and dedication to God. Readings from Scripture may highlight themes of charity, compassion, and the call to live a virtuous life.

Prayer and Devotions:

Devotees and admirers of St. Frances of Rome engage in

personal and communal prayers on her feast day. They may recite prayers specific to her intercession, seeking her guidance and inspiration in their own spiritual journeys.

Reflection on Virtues:

The feast day provides an opportunity for reflection on the virtues exemplified by St. Frances of Rome. Individuals may contemplate her commitment to charity, humility, and a balanced life of prayer and service.

Educational Programs:

Educational institutions, especially those named in honor of St. Frances of Rome, may organize programs and activities that highlight her life and teachings. These initiatives aim to inspire students and promote awareness of her legacy.

Charitable Acts and Service:

Given St. Frances of Rome's dedication to serving the poor, the feast day often involves charitable acts and service projects. Communities may engage in works of mercy, extending assistance to those in need in honor of her compassionate spirit.

Feast Day Meals and Gatherings:

Families and communities may come together for special meals and gatherings to celebrate St. Frances of Rome's feast day. These occasions foster a sense of community and provide an opportunity for fellowship.

Artistic and Cultural Events:

Artistic performances, cultural events, and exhibitions that showcase St. Frances of Rome's life and influence may be organized. These events contribute to a broader understanding of her impact on both religious and cultural realms.

Processions and Pilgrimages:

In certain regions, processions and pilgrimages to shrines or churches dedicated to St. Frances of Rome may take place. Pilgrims express their devotion through these journeys, seeking spiritual enrichment and guidance.

The celebration of St. Frances of Rome's feast day is a multifaceted commemoration that encompasses spiritual, educational, charitable, and communal elements. It serves as a time for believers to draw inspiration from her example and renew their commitment to a life of faith and service.

Traditions and Customs Associated with St. Frances of Rome

The veneration of St. Frances of Rome has given rise to various traditions and customs that reflect the admiration and devotion of her followers. These practices contribute to the celebration of her feast day and the ongoing recognition of her impact on the Catholic Church.

Prayer to St. Frances:

Devotees often engage in specific prayers dedicated to St.

Frances of Rome, seeking her intercession for various intentions. These prayers may be recited individually or as part of communal gatherings, expressing a deep connection with her spiritual presence.

Visits to Shrines and Churches:

Pilgrims and believers may undertake visits to shrines or churches dedicated to St. Frances of Rome. These sacred spaces serve as focal points for prayer, reflection, and seeking her intercession. Pilgrimages may take place on her feast day or throughout the year.

Lighting of Candles:

Lighting candles in honor of St. Frances is a symbolic gesture expressing devotion and seeking spiritual illumination. Candles may be lit in churches, shrines, or personal prayer spaces as a visible sign of the connection with her heavenly intercession.

Feast Day Meals:

Families and communities may observe St. Frances of Rome's feast day by sharing special meals. These gatherings provide an opportunity for fellowship, reflection on her life, and the communal celebration of faith.

Acts of Charity:

In alignment with St. Frances' commitment to charitable works, her feast day may involve organized acts of kindness and service.

Communities engage in works of mercy, extending assistance to the less fortunate as a tangible expression of devotion.

Educational Programs and Lectures:

Institutions named after St. Frances of Rome may organize educational programs, lectures, or seminars on her life and teachings. These events aim to deepen understanding and inspire individuals to incorporate her virtues into their lives.

Processions and Parades:

Some regions may organize processions or parades on St. Frances' feast day. These public events involve the display of religious icons, banners, and symbols associated with her, creating a visible expression of communal devotion.

Artistic Expressions:

Artistic expressions, including paintings, sculptures, and performances, may depict scenes from St. Frances of Rome's life. These creative works contribute to the visual representation of her legacy and inspire contemplation.

Distribution of Devotional Items:

Devotional items such as prayer cards, medals, or blessed objects associated with St. Frances may be distributed during feast day celebrations. These items serve as tangible reminders of her spiritual influence.

Renewal of Commitment:

St. Frances of Rome's feast day may be an occasion for believers to renew their commitment to a life of faith, charity, and prayer. It serves as a time for personal reflection and a rekindling of the desire to emulate her virtues.

These traditions and customs reflect the diverse ways in which individuals and communities express their reverence for St. Frances of Rome and draw inspiration from her exemplary life.

7

Complete Novena

Novena to St. Frances of Rome: Day 1

In the name of the Father, and of the Son, and of the Holy Spirit. Amen.

Day 1: Virtuous Woman of God

O Saint Frances of Rome, virtuous woman of God, you who embraced a life of holiness, charity, and unwavering faith, we turn to you in this novena seeking your intercession.

Reflection:

Today, we reflect on your exemplary virtues. Your commitment to prayer, humility, and serving those in need has left an indelible mark on the Church and inspires us to live lives of virtue and devotion.

Prayer:

St. Frances, you who walked the path of holiness with grace, we ask for your intercession as we strive to emulate your virtues. Pray that we may grow in prayerfulness, humility, and a genuine love for others. Help us, through your example, to draw closer to God and live virtuous lives.

(State your intentions here...)

Our Father, Hail Mary, Glory Be

Closing Prayer:

O Holy Saint Frances of Rome, on this first day of our novena, we entrust our intentions to your intercession. May your virtuous life guide us on our journey of faith. Amen.

In the name of the Father, and of the Son, and of the Holy Spirit. Amen.

Novena to St. Frances of Rome: Day 2

In the name of the Father, and of the Son, and of the Holy Spirit. Amen.

Day 2: Model of Compassion

O Saint Frances of Rome, model of compassion and selfless love, we continue our novena, seeking your intercession and guidance.

Reflection:

Today, we reflect on your compassionate heart, ever open to the needs of others. Your acts of charity and kindness teach us the transformative power of love. Help us to cultivate hearts of compassion in our own lives.

Prayer:

St. Frances, compassionate servant of God, we ask for your intercession as we strive to follow your example. Pray that our hearts may be moved with genuine love for those who are suffering or in need. Help us to be instruments of God's compassion in the world.

(State your intentions here...)

Our Father, Hail Mary, Glory Be

Closing Prayer:

O Holy Saint Frances of Rome, on this second day of our novena, we entrust our intentions to your compassionate intercession. May your love inspire us to reach out to those in need. Amen.

In the name of the Father, and of the Son, and of the Holy Spirit. Amen.

Novena to St. Frances of Rome: Day 3

In the name of the Father, and of the Son, and of the Holy Spirit. Amen.

Day 3: Patroness of Widows

O Saint Frances of Rome, patroness of widows, we turn to you on this third day of our novena, seeking your intercession for those who carry the heavy burden of loss.

Reflection:

Today, we reflect on your empathy and support for widows. Your understanding and compassion brought solace to those who grieved. Pray for all who have experienced the pain of losing a spouse, that they may find comfort in their faith.

Prayer:

St. Frances, compassionate comforter of widows, intercede for those who mourn the loss of their life partners. Ask our Lord to grant them strength, peace, and the assurance of His abiding presence. Help us to be instruments of consolation in their lives.

(State your intentions here...)

Our Father, Hail Mary, Glory Be

Closing Prayer:

O Holy Saint Frances of Rome, on this third day of our novena, we lift up the intentions of those who bear the weight of widowhood.

May your intercession bring them comfort and hope. Amen.

In the name of the Father, and of the Son, and of the Holy Spirit. Amen.

Novena to St. Frances of Rome: Day 4

In the name of the Father, and of the Son, and of the Holy Spirit. Amen.

Day 4: Defender of Family Life

O Saint Frances of Rome, defender of family life, we come before you on this fourth day of our novena, seeking your intercession for all families.

Reflection:

Today, we reflect on your commitment to the sanctity of family life. Your dedication as a wife and mother, rooted in faith, serves as an inspiration. Pray for all families, that they may be strengthened in love, unity, and faith.

Prayer:

St. Frances, model of family virtue, intercede for families around the world. Pray for the grace to navigate challenges with faith and resilience. May the Holy Family be their guide, and may your example inspire them to grow in holiness within the bonds of family.

(State your intentions here...)

Our Father, Hail Mary, Glory Be

Closing Prayer:

O Holy Saint Frances of Rome, on this fourth day of our novena, we entrust all families to your intercession. May they be blessed with love, understanding, and enduring faith. Amen.

In the name of the Father, and of the Son, and of the Holy Spirit. Amen.

Novena to St. Frances of Rome: Day 5

In the name of the Father, and of the Son, and of the Holy Spirit. Amen.

Day 5: Guiding Light in Adversity

O Saint Frances of Rome, guiding light in adversity, we gather on this fifth day of our novena, seeking your intercession for all facing challenges and trials.

Reflection:

Today, we reflect on your steadfastness in times of adversity. Your unwavering faith and trust in God's providence during difficulties inspire us. Pray for all those going through hardships, that they may find strength and courage in their faith.

Prayer:

St. Frances, beacon of hope in adversity, intercede for those in the midst of trials. May they be surrounded by the light of God's love and find the courage to persevere. Help us to trust in God's guidance, even when the path seems uncertain.

(State your intentions here...)

Our Father, Hail Mary, Glory Be

Closing Prayer:

O Holy Saint Frances of Rome, on this fifth day of our novena, we entrust to your intercession all those facing adversity. May they find comfort in God's love and guidance. Amen.

In the name of the Father, and of the Son, and of the Holy Spirit. Amen.

Novena to St. Frances of Rome: Day 6

In the name of the Father, and of the Son, and of the Holy Spirit. Amen.

Day 6: Advocate for the Poor and Afflicted

O Saint Frances of Rome, advocate for the poor and afflicted, we approach you on this sixth day of our novena, seeking your intercession for those in need.

Reflection:

Today, we reflect on your tireless efforts to serve the poor and those facing affliction. Your compassion and dedication inspire us to reach out to the marginalized. Pray for all who suffer, that they may experience the love and care of Christ through our actions.

Prayer:

St. Frances, compassionate advocate for the poor, intercede for those who face poverty, illness, or despair. May we, like you, be moved to alleviate their suffering and work towards justice and mercy. Help us to see the face of Christ in those in need.

(State your intentions here…)

Our Father, Hail Mary, Glory Be

Closing Prayer:

O Holy Saint Frances of Rome, on this sixth day of our novena, we entrust to your intercession all those in need. May your compassion inspire us to be instruments of God's love in the world. Amen.

In the name of the Father, and of the Son, and of the Holy Spirit. Amen.

Novena to St. Frances of Rome: Day 7

In the name of the Father, and of the Son, and of the Holy Spirit. Amen.

Day 7: Intercessor for Spiritual Strength

O Saint Frances of Rome, intercessor for spiritual strength, we come before you on this seventh day of our novena, seeking your guidance in our spiritual journeys.

Reflection:

Today, we reflect on your deep spiritual life, marked by prayer and contemplation. Your connection with God's grace and wisdom serves as a source of inspiration. Pray for us, that we may grow in spiritual strength and draw closer to the heart of God.

Prayer:

St. Frances, model of spiritual resilience, intercede for us as we navigate the challenges of our spiritual lives. May we be anchored in prayer, strengthened by the sacraments, and guided by the Holy Spirit. Help us to persevere in our pursuit of holiness.

(State your intentions here...)

Our Father, Hail Mary, Glory Be

Closing Prayer:

O Holy Saint Frances of Rome, on this seventh day of our novena, we seek your intercession for spiritual strength. May our hearts be open to God's grace, and may we grow ever closer to Him. Amen.

In the name of the Father, and of the Son, and of the Holy Spirit. Amen.

Novena to St. Frances of Rome: Day 8

In the name of the Father, and of the Son, and of the Holy Spirit. Amen.

Day 8: Guide for Humility and Obedience

O Saint Frances of Rome, guide for humility and obedience, we gather on this eighth day of our novena, seeking your intercession for the virtues of humility and obedience in our lives.

Reflection:

Today, we reflect on your humble acceptance of God's will and your obedient response to His call. Your example teaches us the transformative power of humility and the grace that comes from surrendering to God's plan. Pray for us, that we may embrace humility and obedience in our daily lives.

Prayer:

St. Frances, exemplar of humility and obedience, intercede for us as we seek to align our wills with God's divine plan. Help us to cultivate humility in our hearts and to joyfully embrace obedience to His commands. May our lives be a reflection of God's love and wisdom.

(State your intentions here...)

Our Father, Hail Mary, Glory Be

Closing Prayer:

O Holy Saint Frances of Rome, on this eighth day of our novena, we entrust to your intercession our desire for humility and obedience. May we learn from your example and draw closer to God through these virtues. Amen.

In the name of the Father, and of the Son, and of the Holy Spirit. Amen.

Novena to St. Frances of Rome: Day 9

In the name of the Father, and of the Son, and of the Holy Spirit. Amen.

Day 9: Seeker of Divine Wisdom

O Saint Frances of Rome, seeker of divine wisdom, we come to the final day of our novena, seeking your intercession for the wisdom to discern God's will in our lives.

Reflection:

Today, we reflect on your deep desire for divine wisdom and understanding. Your life was marked by a profound connection with God's guidance. Pray for us, that we may be granted the gift of wisdom to navigate life's complexities with discernment and grace.

Prayer:

St. Frances, wise and discerning servant of God, intercede for us as we seek the wisdom that comes from above. Help us to discern God's will in our lives, to make choices that align with His plan, and to grow in spiritual understanding. May we be receptive to the promptings of the Holy Spirit.

(State your intentions here...)

Our Father, Hail Mary, Glory Be

Closing Prayer:

O Holy Saint Frances of Rome, on this final day of our novena, we humbly place our intentions before you, seeking divine wisdom. May your intercession guide us on the path of God's will, and may we be blessed with the wisdom to discern and follow His plan for our lives. Amen.

In the name of the Father, and of the Son, and of the Holy Spirit. Amen.

Final Prayer to St. Frances of Rome

O Holy Saint Frances of Rome, faithful servant of God and exemplar of virtue, we conclude this novena with hearts filled with gratitude for your intercession and inspiration.

You, who lived a life marked by profound humility, compassion, and a deep connection with the divine, have guided us in our reflections and prayers. We thank you for your example of holiness and your tireless dedication to God's will.

As we have traversed these nine days seeking your intercession, we entrust to you our intentions, both spoken and unspoken. Please present them to our merciful God, who knows the desires of our hearts.

St. Frances, may your unwavering faith, your love for the poor, your humility, and your obedience to God's will continue to inspire us on our spiritual journey. Help us to live lives that reflect the beauty of holiness and draw us closer to our Creator.

We ask for your continued intercession, that we may be granted the virtues of wisdom, compassion, and humility in our daily lives. Pray for us, O beloved saint, that we may follow in your footsteps and grow in holiness.

We conclude this novena in the name of the Father, and of the Son, and of the Holy Spirit. Amen.

St. Frances of Rome, pray for us.

8

Conclusion

Lasting Impression

St. Frances of Rome, through her life of profound virtue, charity, and unwavering faith, leaves a lasting impression that resonates through the corridors of time. Her legacy endures, imprinting hearts and minds with several key aspects that continue to inspire:

Holiness in Daily Life:

St. Frances' life teaches us that holiness is not confined to grand gestures but is found in the simplicity of everyday actions. Her commitment to prayer, humility, and service reflects a path to sanctity accessible to all.

Balancing Contemplation and Action:

The harmonious blend of contemplative prayer and active service demonstrated by St. Frances challenges the notion of a dichotomy between a life of prayer and engagement with the world. Her example encourages us to integrate both aspects for a holistic spiritual journey.

Compassion for the Vulnerable:

St. Frances' compassion for the poor, sick, and widowed stands as a timeless model. Her dedication to alleviating the suffering of others reflects the call to embody Christ's love through acts of mercy and solidarity with the marginalized.

Family as a Source of Holiness:

As a devoted wife and mother, St. Frances emphasizes the sanctity of family life. Her commitment to her family serves as a reminder that the domestic sphere is a fertile ground for spiritual growth and virtue.

Patronage for Specific Concerns:

St. Frances' designation as the patroness of motorists and widows underscores her relevance to contemporary concerns. Her patronage extends to aspects of daily life, emphasizing her intercessory role in practical matters.

Spiritual Writings and Teachings:

St. Frances' spiritual writings provide a reservoir of wisdom. Her reflections on prayer, humility, and devotion offer a guide for those seeking to deepen their spiritual lives and draw closer to God.

Innovation in Religious Life:

The foundation of the Oblates of Mary, with its unique combination of contemplative and active elements, showcases St. Frances' innovative approach to religious life. Her vision continues to influence religious communities seeking a dynamic balance.

Enduring Patronage and Feast Day Celebration:

The continued recognition of St. Frances as the patroness of various concerns and the annual celebration of her feast day attests to the enduring impact of her life. Believers turn to her intercession, finding inspiration and solace.

In essence, St. Frances of Rome leaves an indelible mark, inviting each generation to embrace a life of holiness, compassion, and devotion. Her legacy serves as a timeless testament to the transformative power of faith lived out in love for God and neighbor.

Continued Reverence

The continued reverence for St. Frances of Rome manifests in various ways, reflecting the enduring impact of her life and virtues:

Devotional Practices:

Believers worldwide maintain devotional practices dedicated

to St. Frances. Prayerful invocations, the lighting of candles, and visits to shrines or churches named in her honor stand as expressions of ongoing veneration.

Feast Day Celebrations:

The annual celebration of St. Frances of Rome's feast day on March 9th remains a focal point for Catholics and admirers. Communities come together in prayer, reflection, and acts of charity to commemorate her life and seek her intercession.

Inclusion in Liturgical Calendar:

St. Frances' inclusion in the liturgical calendar ensures that her memory is perpetually acknowledged within the Catholic Church. This liturgical recognition underscores her significance as a model of holiness.

Educational Endeavors:

Institutions named after St. Frances of Rome often integrate her life and teachings into educational programs. Students and scholars engage with her legacy, drawing inspiration from her virtues and contributions to spirituality.

Religious Communities:

Religious communities, particularly the Oblates of Mary founded by St. Frances, continue to uphold her innovative approach to religious life. The enduring presence of these communities attests to the sustainability of her vision.

Patronage for Specific Concerns:

The designation of St. Frances as the patroness of motorists, widows, and other specific concerns ensures a continued reliance on her intercession in various aspects of daily life. People turn to her for guidance and protection.

Artistic Depictions:

Artistic representations, including paintings and sculptures depicting scenes from St. Frances' life, contribute to the visual commemoration of her legacy. These artistic expressions serve as reminders of her enduring impact.

Spiritual Writings:

St. Frances' spiritual writings, preserved and studied, continue to inspire readers seeking insights into prayer, humility, and the contemplative life. Her words offer a timeless source of guidance for those on the spiritual journey.

In essence, the continued reverence for St. Frances of Rome reflects a recognition of her sanctity and the ongoing relevance of her example. As individuals and communities turn to her in prayer and celebration, they draw strength and inspiration from the profound legacy she left behind.

Printed in Great Britain
by Amazon